Transmissions from Bone House

Transmissions from Bone House

Stephen Bunch

Woodley Memorial Press

Edited by Al Ortolani
Copy Editing by Melissa Fite Johnson

Book design: Cami Travis-Groves
Cover Art: "Spirit Lines," collage by Barbara Solberg,
www.bsolbergart.com

Woodley Press
Department of English
Washburn University
Topeka, KS 66621

ISBN: 978-0-9908128-6-9

This one's for Joy.

Acknowledgments

My thanks to the editors of the publications in which the following poems previously appeared:

"The Eumenides" and "The Program" in *Autumn Sky Poetry*

"Blues for an Identity Thief" and "Election" in *The Externalist*

"Five Retablos" and "News from the Ultra Deep Field" in *Fickle Muses*

"Still" in *IthacaLit: Lit with Art* and *Rootdrinker: Trade Goods*

"Two Blues for Odysseus" in *IthacaLit: Lit with Art* and *Tellus*

"White World" in *IthacaLit: Lit with Art*

"The Daily Entrails," "A Recent Survey," and "Second Life" in *Mudlark*

"Aliens" and "The Bone" in *Phantom Kangaroo*

"Alias" in *Touch: A Journal of Healing*

I also wish to thank Melissa Fite Johnson for her impeccable proofreading, Cami Travis-Groves for design, and Al Ortolani for his editorial expertise (and patience) in ushering this project to its conclusion.

Special thanks to Donald Levering, whose counsel was crucial when the book was still a work in progress; to Mike Harrell for his careful reading, questioning, and encouragement; to Denise Low, Sherry O'Keefe, and William Slaughter for their ongoing support; and to Barbara Solberg, whose hand and eye continue to delight.

Contents

1

3

4

The Program

No witness is protected.
Some who see
drop from sight.
Others remain visible
but go blind or mad.
You may be confined to your house,
the stainless kitchen waiting
with sharp edges, your sleep broken by rats
gnawing in bedroom walls.
You may retire to a rotting climate, a
corrupt latitude of rainy afternoons
and thick starless nights.
Weeks may pass, or years,
before you are called.
Or the call may never come.
But each time the telephone rings
you will remember
what you saw.
You will close your eyes
and answer.

Blues for an Identity Thief

Your mother didn't know you
when you returned. The dog
snapped at you. The bur oak
by the driveway had changed
into a hedgerow while you were gone.
Without the map in the glovebox
you never would have found
your hometown
or the right street.
Even now you can't name your old school
or your sister's husband.
In another city, on a different map,
your wife sleeps in a house
you can't describe. You can barely
imagine her face or remember
the children, their birthdays, their voices.

Your wallet is filled with pictures of strangers,
but when you stopped for the siren,
the officer noted the likeness
in the driver's license photo
and wrote you a ticket in another man's name.
Fines, he said, can be paid by phone
with a valid credit card
and a contrite heart.
One out of two isn't bad, you heard
yourself say, then put the citation away,
and unfolded yet another man's map.

When your cell phone chattered,
someone else answered
before sitting down to your dinner.

Orientation

Here is a telephone directory.
Find yourself.

Here is a window.
Look out.

Or in.
You decide.

This calendar can give a clue
if you know when to start.

Listen for the tread
of the mail carrier
on the porch, the rattle
of the mailbox.
Then see whose name
is on the letter.

If time allows, go
to the emergency room
to have your entrails reckoned.
When the x-rays arrive
frame them and hang them
on the bedroom wall.

Sit in this armchair and get
to know your elbows.

The worn path in the carpet
is your life till now.
Keep walking.

Aliens

They have been here all along,
not Andromedans or even Mexicans.
They conduct experiments on their spouses,
abduct their children,
drive the whole family to Disney World.
They build slab houses and gated estates,
five-star restaurants and liquor stores with
drive-thru windows,
not pyramids or sidereal stelai
or interstellar bridges.
If they were telepathic they'd know
we don't need mind readers, that each
of us is the other, they'd know
their own shadowy thoughts
and despair of returning home.

The Eumenides

Every night the murderers cruise the neighborhood.
Sometimes they wield golf clubs, sometimes Uzis
or canisters of gas or syringes dripping
heart attacks. Their headlights
shine down the cul-de-sac and back,
leaving a cloud of sweet exhaustion.

They call themselves harvesters
and comb the mowed lawns
with footsteps heavy as the odor
of four-o'clocks opening at dusk.
We call them hellhounds, keep the doors
locked till dawn, try to sleep without dreaming.

With daylight we make coffee, step
outside for the news, walk dogs,
go to work. Most mornings we won't notice
the ambulance stopped down the street,
lights flashing, or the crime scene tape
as it catches the sun in its latest tangle.

Day Trader

Full of years, I have traded
my days away, sold my shares
to circadian pulsings of hope
and fear. I have spent my life
in arbitrage among the border people,
have grown into the knowledge of edges
and learned the comfort of lines,
of crossings and returns.
Now the pages of this book of days
turn from the margins inward
on names and numbers,
verses and reverses, folded
for the morning when word
becomes flesh again, the market
opens, and the bidding begins.

A Recent Survey

"More than half can't find heart on body diagram"
—CNN headline

More than half of us can't find our hearts
and don't know the shape of our lungs.
But most of us know where our guts take up space
and can pick out intestines in a lineup of innards.

All but a few, men and women alike, know
the penis, though its importance splits
opinions along gender lines.
On the other hand only a slight majority
admits much knowledge of clitoral matters.
Most support further research.

Respondents were unanimous
in having no spleen, and no one can name
the four humors anymore.
We know, however, "the neck bone's
connected to the back bone,"
and some among us
"hear the word of the Lord"
even if ignorant of dem
auditory ossicles.

The Blog Index

At the end of March
talk of death peaked.
Birth, marriage, taxes
were steady whispers,
nothing more.
Even as the chatter of tax
deadlines and June weddings
spiked,
our conversations and soliloquies
kept bending back
like iron shavings to the magnet
of ultimate things.
By September
death was approaching previous highs,
taxes had made a modest rebound,
talk of birth and marriage
came from voices shut in distant rooms.

Data

Like speech balloons in comics,
words and their products
have moved into a cloud,
all memories, affections, dogma,
distractions, a digital condensate
to rain or dissipate,
all thought lost at last.

Approximation[1] from Cuneiform Found on a Neolithic Bowl [2]

Deep inside winter we clean
and sharpen our tools[3],
preparing to carry them
into new sunlight.

Where we live the atmosphere
is red and translucent.
Our blood is never farther
than a casual thought[4] from the surface.

Each summer we emerge
with hopeless optimism[5],
stabbing shovels into crust,
swinging bright blades against dark growth.

Soon enough the roots and branches
will forget[6] us, and then we will be gone[7,8].

1   This piece is not intended as translation as it is thrice removed from the original cuneiform. Instead, it is meant to be a poem derived from an English translation, which itself was derived from a German rendering of the original Arabic translation of the cuneiform glyphs.

2   Archaeologists have been unable to determine if the bowl was used ceremonially, in food preparation, for storage, or for some other unknown purpose.

3   The glyph rendered "sharpen our tools" also could be taken to mean "sharpen our weapons," but the later agricultural references suggest the former (although what I have presented as "dark growth" could be any of the following: "forest," "the enemy," or "nightmares").

4   Regarding "casual thought," parts of the inscription are worn, leading the original translator, Egyptian archaeologist Saul bin Said, to suggest that this glyph could represent "sleep" or "consciousness" or, alternatively, "a wound."

5   "Hopeless optimism" may seem an oxymoron, although I would suggest that it makes a certain fatalistic sense, the optimism needed for day-to-day living, the hopelessness an acknowledged awareness. The first of the two glyphs behind this phrase means something like "the sun always sets." The second means "the sun always rises."

6   From a graduate student's translation of a transcription of a tape-recorded interview with Professor bin Said: "We cannot know if the abstract phenomenon of 'forgetting' was recognized 'consciously' in Neolithic spoken languages or in the cuneiform, and the glyph in question could as easily represent [garbled] of a line drawn in [garbled] or 'growth' or 'a dark [garbled]....' A translator is constantly reminded of the [garbled] of knowing."

7   The anonymous English translation from which I have created this "approximation" was found in a collection of as yet uncatalogued papers, the provenance of which is uncertain, held by the Spencer Research Library at the University of Kansas. The paper on which the translation was handwritten has what appear to be coffee stains obscuring the last few words. I have had to take liberties in my treatment of this final clause, relying in part on the "best guess" recorded in the previous note and on my sense that the bowl's inscription was meant as a kind of memento mori, a reminder of human mutability. Being a scholar of neither Neolithic cultures nor cuneiform, I admit the possible, even likely, fallibility of my word choices both in the final clause and throughout this "approximation."

8   HTTP Error 404 - File Not Found.

Cloud(e)scape

The data have been raptured
leaving the earth()bound clueless,
no GIS, no inferences to be drawn,
no influences, no inductions,
all evaporation.

The digital currency has also ascended.
The poor are with us always, left broke
and behind, as prophets and profits
have long since soared
through the widening hole in the ozone.

Even the eagles have tired of dining
on redeeming Promethean liver,
even the appetite for torment finds
no satisfaction on this forsaken cairn.

Cell

Voices hold you hostage.
Conversation keeps you in stir.
You are never alone.
Your calls may be monitored
but only you can hear
the whispers of your accusers
in the scraping of plaque and platelets
pulsing in your ears.
You are always alone,
and the sleepers know where you live
in the metastatic silence,
your words breaking
up, your sentences
locked down.

Crawlspace

In the newspaper today:
Paranoia on the rise.

No hostile takeovers here
but no light either,
or rather a dusty brown
luminous gauze.

No new toxins, just the old ones
put down when the lumber
bled out, expired insulation,
cadmium from the plumber's torch.

Near the corner by the window well
the port bottles the painters left,
the box of bones, smooth,
cleaned in time's solvent.

No labyrinthine plots in years,
just children hiding,
waiting for the old ones
to come looking.

City Limits

The darkness rattles with vandals
shaking latches all over town.
Sleepers shatter glass with their snoring.
Moonlight hums and sputters on rooftops.

Refugees clog the exits,
the old ones fleeing desire,
the young ones full of it,
opened up, in the night air.

Two Blues for Odysseus

1

No Man I,
no nomen,
no men, one
alone, all
one, no
nombre, Nemo,
no hombre,
no mo'.

2

Unseen is not
invisible, unheard
not silent,
always looking,
listening,
never resting,
sea-rise, landfall,
seer's eyes, all
ears, all hands
forgetting, no man
remembered.

2

Brain Scan

An aerial view reveals
islands in the blood,

strata of distress, depressed
landscape.

The dizzying fall was not
recorded, the nausea not

recognized. Now
the klaxons are embedded

somewhere in memory,
the jackhammers, the storm

warnings. No worries—
it's there at birth

just waiting
to be found.

Djurnal

The weight at waking presses
down against the rising of the day. The cracks
in the plaster expand and contract as the
house moves with the hilltop
swell of limestone and clay, oscillations
of past and present, not much traction
for divination. Still, I stare at these fissures
as I lie in bed, sure there must be meaning there.
The world we now know keeps ending,
but imperceptibly. We say we "know it
in our bones," but the cracks close and open,
the diastole dips and rises as certainly
as the diurnal solar entrance and exit.
Words form and then fade
into phonemes then vapor at each exhalation.
A basket of coins rests on the nightstand,
an even or odd collection of heads and tails,
next to a daybook of rectos and versos
mostly blank or abandoned.
Take it or leave it.
None of these things is knowable.
Nothing is negotiable.

Unease

I lie awake waiting for the dogs,
their nightly communiqués
across the alley, all over town.
I know they're talking about me.
The gas main hisses
and a refrigerator truck idles below.
This week's prisoners in the county jail,
down the street, are displayed, backlit,
behind glass, performing in dumb show
to cicadas and hymns from the Salvation Army.
The stars stand still in their places
above this ramshackle house of nerves.

Old Year

The list of suicides lengthens.
They seldom leave notes anymore,

and those who remain
wouldn't read them anyway.

Gravity still obtains,
and the strange comfort of static

on the radio, the drone
of a ventilator through the night.

3 A.M.

A woman's voice contains my name.
Still, I listen to be
released, to be
remembered.

Accommodations

A bathroom faucet drips.
The sound downstairs may be a rat.
The newspaper shrinks daily.
I have learned to live

with the cracked mirror,
the arthritic toe, unread books,
and every desire.

Paint flakes from the ceiling.
I know where the pockets
of dry rot are, this place at last
more familiar than my face.

Night Watch

Bats emerge and bob in the dusk.
A young rabbit screams, caught
in the rapture of an owl.
Inside, the clocks breathe hours
in and out, and the air
conditioner coughs and sighs.

Separation

The extraction of coffee parts sleep
from waking, the morning
a distillation from darkness.
In dreams the child is abandoned
by parents, and the man returns
to the house where his children
once lived, where husband
and wife shared and divided
a life. The newborn emerges,
mother and child beginning
a lifelong divergence, the universe
expanding beyond light's reach.

Trains of Thought

I lie awake listening,
hearing the dark trains
nearing and receding.
The sound separates
the air and the air
dilutes the sound
as language divides
the world,
enables thought but
always falls apart
in the end.

Awake

Someone has expunged
the line between there

and here,
but eyewitnesses

can't agree when
or where

the erasure occurred.
The garbage men sing

far into the morning.
I would sleep

even farther
if I knew how.

Insurgents

Deer conspire in shadows along the roadside,
plotting suicidal leaps into bug-blurred windshields.
Rabbits converge on neighborhood gardens,
leaving stems chewed and twisted with their passage.
At night a forty-pound raccoon
claws a five-hundred-dollar hole in the roof,
and the termites continue their subversion in silence.
Kudzu crawls across the landscape
as a new crash of blue jays slams the panes each day.
Cicadas beam their sine waves against every eardrum
like a dentist's drill in the local jawbone.
At sunrise the chorus of crows mounts again,
twice as loud as yesterday,
tree limbs cracking with their black cries.

300 Grams

When the sleeper wakes to the daily
autopsy, he feels the weight of his heart
as if it were in his hand, the weight
of a glass of water run cold
from the tap. The morning
breeze subsides, time thickens, trees
filter daylight into a cloudy tea,
as if the sun pulsed and strained
through every vein of every leaf, as if
the waking could weigh this day
as if it were the last, could tell
when the sun stopped beating.

Election

He knows angels
live under the wallpaper.
He hears the singing as it weaves its way
through floral patterns and water stains,
strained hosannas thickening the air.

The ceiling lowers as the sun
rises. Shadows sink
into the worn grain of floorboards.

Boxcars rattle beyond his window.
His windows rattle when he sleeps,
disturbing a spider's spinning
behind tired curtains.
But he seldom sleeps.

If he had a table he would sit there.
If he had a chair.
Instead, he stays in bed,
switching the remote
from the candidates' debates
to the quest for monster eels in Canada,
from an equally elusive Holy Grail
to the story of a Nazi bunker
converted to a disco.

And tomorrow will be like today,
only later. Yesterday's sandwich

will remain uneaten on the mattress.
He will close his eyes and listen
to the weeds growing in a garden
he almost remembers.
In the damp smells rising
from storm sewers,
he will hear the ringing
of church bells.

The Elegist

He pieced together the poems for years.
A phrase overheard across a room
would put down roots
and bloom while he slept.

A description read on a café menu
would whisper back long after
the andouille-crusted catfish had passed
from his body's knotted memory.

Dream flotsam washed up in the morning's
coffee cup, a list of regrets, things done
and undone, a fragment of understanding
circled by a string of broken words.

He resolved the annual snowfalls
into invented alphabets, discovered
in the seasons a mathematics of habit,
a linear regression of the flesh.

He pieced together in poems his years,
knowing full well the jail's first prisoner
is often its builder, drunk and disorderly,
sleeping it off in his cell.

3

Alias

The hands before me
are not my hands.
This voice has never been mine.
I've told my stories so many times
I no longer believe them.
Each night I leave,
each morning return, changed,
forgetful, diminished.
Whose smoke am I becoming,
whose ashes?

Signals

I awoke this morning with no hands
to arrange the word blocks,
no way to manipulate
the dawn into thought.
The carillon's notes dissolved in the fog.
The fog dissolved into daylight.
Children's voices rose from a well.

The extremities are not misnamed
but parts of the expanding universe,
more distant every time I depend
on them, satellites signaling
increasingly unreliable
data, fading,
no help on the way.

Heat Signature

I'm here
in a snowdrift,
under the covers,

radiant yet,
but fading,
waiting to be found.

Proteins fluoresce.
Fingerprints settle
beneath the dust.

Breath condenses
on a pocket mirror.
A pulse still murmurs.

Some look for signs
of life, the rest
for bodies.

Spring Haircut

The scissors clack
and clutches of hair drop
to the sink, shoulders, floor.
Blood rises from the cut on the neck.

Dry ghosts of last year's morning glories
scrape against the bathroom window.
Dogs gather in the alley
sorting the trash.
Snow sinks into the earth.

Sunlight flashes off
the scissors in the mirror.
Thick curls fall from the head
in the mirror.
Ears burn in the light.

A month goes by
before the hair is gone,
turned in the compost
with coffee grounds, eggshells,
asleep in the leaf slime, to be
a memory twined
in next year's bean vines.

Leavings

Outside a dusting
of snow, inside a snowing
of dust, no one home.

The Bone

Where did you find it?
In a field near my father's house.

Did the flesh still cling to it?
It was picked clean, bleached, dry.

Were you afraid?
I picked it up.

What did you feel?
Revulsion and pride.

What will you do with it?
I'll braid my hair with it

or hold it when I sleep.
May I touch it?

Never, you may
never touch it.

White World

It begins with the snow,
the teeth, and the linens,
then the yellowing of urine,
and years,
and yearning.

Procter and Gamble sells
protection, the pastes and gels
and suds, but the taint
settles into the bones.

The lost whiteness of phosphorus
leaves the aging soil infertile,
transforms detergents
into Luciferian bearers of light

and death by napalm for the yellow-
skinned people, with its "ability
to penetrate deeply...
into the musculature, where
it would continue to burn
day after day."*

But no amount of scrubbing
or fire from the skies
can expunge the middle passage
or blood stains under hanging trees
and street lights

after sugar cane pulled the light
from Caribbean soil into rum
exchanged for dark people.

We aspire to a white world,
the absence of troubling color,
and we leave yellowed teeth and bones.

* Lindqvist, Sven (2001). *A History of Bombing*

The Daily Entrails

Hope is the thing
on the grill—bled out,
plucked, smoldering—
fit to be consumed
in a fit of hunger,
then deposited
with all the other offal,
the sludge and slurry,
leaving unchanged,
hovering, that other
thing with feathers,
that drooling
buzzard, worry.

Five Retablos

1

Lord of small disappointments,
you stand beside an empty mailbox,
an egg with broken yolk
in the skillet that tips
from your drooping left hand.
In the upraised palm
of your right hand rests
a crumpled lottery ticket.
Behind you the grass
needs cutting.

2

Lord of forgiveness, lord
of the open door, your welcome
mat is out, the wine
uncorked. You wink
at us and nod toward
the tethered fatted calf
readied for slaughter.

3

Lord of forgetfulness, clothed
in a robe with a dozen empty pockets,
on the ground around you

a shopping list, a ring
of keys, a birthday card,
an old photo of a young
man. Your face
is blurred and your fist
grips tight a bouquet,
forget-me-nots for no one
in memoriam.

4

Lord of no fortune, your silver
sunglasses hide snake eyes
but mirror the aces and eights
that bloom in one hand
and the credit cards fanned
in the other. In the background
is a harbor, on the horizon a ship
so small who can tell
if it's coming in
or setting sail. Our Lady
stands beside you, flips
a coin, and smiles.

5

Lord of sorrows, hands
outstretched, empty, wounded
eyes, the weeping
shake of shoulders in off-
the-rack sackcloth.
You will not protect us

from ourselves,
and you will not prevent us
from praying. You open
your arms as if saying
"I have nothing, I have
nothing here for you."

Fallen

Natural systems are changing faster than thought systems.
—from a notebook

Lucifer descends before Luna.
The *via lactea* curdles unseen beyond the lighted carbon veil.
Phosphorous concentrates in aging soil.
The landscape gives up a weakening pulse.
Only bones remain as guideposts to Paradise,
only bones and a trail of rotting fruit.

News from the Ultra Deep Field

Odysseus drinks alone
in a bar in Topeka.
Over the horizon of his glass,
the television hovers, muted,
flashing pictures from the Hubble,
images from the Beginning
of Time, says the crawler
along the bottom of the screen.
The one-eyed bartender
winks knowingly. Or blinks
unwittingly. Who can tell?
The universe expands as Odysseus
chews an ice cube,
but the distance on the interstate
from Salina to Kansas City
does not change,
and truckers travel through
the void of a prairie night
not hearing the sirens.
On a plateau in New Mexico,
the Very Large Array
listens for news of the Wanderer,
somewhere between Ilium and Ithaca,
somewhere beyond the gradual
ascent of the high plains,
sometime before last call.

The Illusion

Without it the blues would blast
from every frequency on the radio dial,
wash over the shoppers in every mall,
ring out from minarets and campaniles,
indifferent to clocks and calendars.

Grammar would make no sense,
logic become a will o' the wisp.
Telephones would fall silent
and the Internet cease spinning its web.

The sanitation department would stop
its weekly prowl, sirens would halt
their senseless howl, and the sleepers
would startle themselves awake.

Unscrambling an Egg

"When you break an egg and scramble it you are doing cosmology."
—*Sean Carroll, California Institute of Technology*

Eventually an egg will emerge scrambled
never having been broken
in the faint crackling at the edge of a universe
overcrowded with absentees.

Sometime afterward or before
a yolk will separate from albumen,
coalesce in a shell,
probably unobserved.

Words will fall apart and precipitate,
break into brittle sounds, lines and dots,
chicken scratches, brief fluorescences,
closing and opening hatches.

Last Things

One receding bar of soap,
its wrapper recycled a week ago,

an old voice retained for years
on an answering machine,

the weight of one fingerprint, of everything
learned, every sadness, every fearless

or compassionate act,
the exhalation of all

knowledge and memory, morning
fog in river bottoms.

Song

Separate the coffee from
the morning
the rain from the broken
glass the
broken glass beneath the trees
from the
leaves rotting behind the nostrils

Separate the cause from
effect
come for me come
for me when
the moon
come for me when the moon
shines black
through the light of the window

Still

Under the moonscape of the bedroom
ceiling you lowered yourself
onto me, brushed my lips with your breast, then
pressed your finger there, whispered,
"Don't wake the baby,"

and outside
in the meadow where the glacier stopped
moving millennia ago
one lone boulder stood silent, lost,
and in the dust and crushed rock of the driveway
chamomile clung to the earth's crust and flowered.

You rolled your hips with the light's
changes from the cumuli and the curtains, with
the reluctant breeze through
the window screen, the cool
rhythm of a lawn sprinkler down
the road what seemed a season ago

but as current as the unattended jazz
playing from the radio in the next room
through closed doors that afternoon
and still.

Station Identification

You will know me by my
frequency, by the sequence of numbers
I recite as you wait for sleep.
You will know me by the distance
between us on a clear night.
Do not rely on my voice, which changes
its shape with each syllable.
Satellites blanket the planet
with a blind man's blues.
The air fills with signals and wonders.
If you receive me you'll think that
you know me. Stay tuned.

4

Second Life

*"The curtain might rise
anywhere on a single speaker"*—Edward Dorn

1

In the beginning, we're told, was
the Word, as told by The Word,
and the rest is History,
as the saying goes—
remains, leftovers, to pick
through, recycle, take
apart, reassemble.

The settlers here live in logos cabins
built by linkin' blogs
from the Great Emancipator,
in a chain of being that beggars
any known epistemology.

Above the road to Bone House
a young woman hovers
in her solar-powered levitation vest.
She, as most of us, has
known only the rapture of two suns,
the paradisal parade,
not that old Antaean grounding—

but this is no narrative. I have

no story to tell. No one's life
is an arc. The only plot
lies somewhere off the road
to Bone House, and even
She Who Hovers cannot descry
it or, left alone, describe.

2

My mother won a freezer and a fur
coat on Queen for a Day one year,
back when we had
just the one sun—

that's not a story either, only
accidents in succession.
She filled in three blanks:

In Bosch's Hell a rat [pounds a drum]. Ding.

[Marlon Brando] said, "I don't like
the country. Crickets
make me nervous."
Ding ding.

On Bolivar Peninsula, Hurricane Ike
revealed a football-sized
[mammoth's tooth].
Ding ding ding.

Each blank could have been a story,
but she was no narrator, rather
a filler of factual gaps
(and she stored the fur coat [in the freezer]).

3

If this accounting were a story,
it would probably trace the roamings
of the human genome, the hiphopping
Y and the independent, dependable
X. But these characters need no N[arrator],
as billiard balls need no cue,
at most an interpreter, someone

who can excavate the foundation of
Bone House, beyond which now
our two suns set, or explicate
the narratives of the Tenders of Lies
importuning at every crossroad—
But that, too, begins to sound
like a story, even a meta-
story, crackling in the electronic thicket.

4

In Second Life the Hall of Lectures
accepts into it a colorful assembly,
not individuals but clusters
of behavior seeking a plan or
if not a plan a mode or
an organizing principle.

They view the Lecturer from different
angles, without knowing angles, and hear
his voice on different wavelengths
while parsing his words into a thousand
different understandings.
Each thinks he knows

but all hear the scraping of the backhoe
back at Bone House where
the Programmer prepares to backdate
the cornerstone when it sees
sunslight—

which again is no story, a mere fact
made up for convenience, a fabrication
like any stone carved to purpose
or not—

5

much like the unicorns released
to the countryside by the sentimental
and unimaginative, which have multiplied,
much as do also the sentimental
and unimaginative, trampling
the red wheat and despoiling the forests—

all of which too could pass for narrative
on a sunsless day, though the details
likely would muffle interest,
so many alleles turned
to such obscure ends.

Perhaps after breakfast someone will
unleash a pack of teenage boys
with laser blasters to thin the herd,
which at least would be a linear gesture
if not a story's line.

6

When the suns eventually set,
the iDream (patent pending) captures
the citizens' subconscious.
They plug in to download
their nocturnal transmissions
for playback when they wake.
They swap the narratives with friends
or deposit them in Dream Bank boxes
on even-numbered and oddly-
named streets and wait
for interest to accrue.

Everyone knows by word
of mouth whose dreams are best.
iDream Editor is in beta test.

7

In First Life, Dr. Aribert Heim
collected *Jüdische Schädel,*
especially treasured the children's skulls
in a line on a shelf
in his Mauthausen office.
Somewhere they went missing,
as did he from the photograph
of his German champion hockey team,
ten years post-war.
The Khazars, he claimed, drove him
to the tennis court roof of the rundown hotel

in downtown Cairo. They forced him to hear
the muezzein's call from Al Azhar Mosque,
to which he walked fifteen miles each day,
Tarek Hussein Farid, with the check
from his sister in Baden-Baden
and his German Koran, gift
for Uncle Tarek
from his landlord's children.

Seldom seen in Cairo's streets and stalls
without his camera, he never appeared
in a photograph. His unpublished
book on the Zionists disappeared
in Second Life, as did his cancer-
ridden Aryan body.

8

"NeXT," say the letters
on the vacated building in Redwood City,
the one with I.M. Pei's

((((((floating staircase))))))

Now it's an inpost for skunks and rodents,
raccoons and foxes,
feral cats.

If every narrative needs a next,
then the previous NeXT is Now,
after the Gold Rush has doffed its Levi's
and plucked its chickens,
after the Silver Surfer
has washed up on the silicon strand,
as RejuVimed shores up
the foundation,
anchors the staircase—
voila! *vivarium.*

9

And so it begins again, another
iteration, recombinant in the retelling,
running on the inside track, another
accident needing to happen, another
avatar flipping switches
cut from the family tree.

[Reload current page]

My avatar blogs about my life—

Stephen has 63 friends,
but they're not speaking—

and others' avatars read it
as if my life is all middle,
no beginning and end.
Chances are my avatar
will outlive me,
but he'll run out of things to blog about,
if he hasn't already, since verbs
and adverbs and pre-
positions and prepossessions
have no place
in Second Life,

and the number of names,
while great, is finite, and
conjunctions become wearisome
after a spell, or even before it's cast,

spellcheck or no.

(Or was that a rumor unleashed
by some other writer about the verbs,
and adverbs and cetera,
disinformation manufactured by
MFA program insurgents. Hmmm?)

Stephen is having leftovers
for dinner
again.

[Reload current page]

404 Error: File not found

[Reload current page]

10

The Speaker of Facts emits messages
from wireless receivers mounted
on each hitching post
all around Town Square
to counter the neigh sayers
and keep the populace in line.

"Peanuts are legumes," the Voice
asserts for the record. "Water
was available yesterday."

On the reality show *Scriptorium Idol*,
monks from various religious traditions
compete to rewrite the classics
to conform to the world we imagine today

(which should not be confused
with the competing program,
Reality Today, flowing through
a pharmaceutical distribution
channel near you).

The audience favorite, a Trappist,
reworks Hemingway—and who wouldn't
want that task—so now, at last,
The Suns Also Rise.
The long shot Gnostic scrivener
has *Ecclesiastes,*
in which no thing is new
under either sun,

though Bone House
must undergo reverse engineering.
The facts change, but the meanings remain
in dispute beyond any
serious lingering
interest.

11

The tour guide at the Memorial for Forgotten Phrases
explains that in the old days
"laughing out loud" meant "LOL."
"We're told," she continues, "that no one ever
wrote or said 'laughing out loud,'
but apparently the phrase existed
before its current transliteration."

"On your right is 'For what it's worth,'
which was a popular song in First Life.
No one knows why it became our 'FWIW,'
despite extensive research on the song's lyrics,
which, FWIW, do not contain the phrase."

She pauses. "If this is TMI,
you may take notes."

12

Do you wish to overwrite this file?
All information will be lost—

unlike palimpsests, in which multiple
stories play out simultaneously, though
some be hidden or infuse their color into the pre-
and post-scripted narratives
cohabiting a parchment.
These scribblers had no fear

[The Speaker of Facts announces: "Today the sky
fills the eye."]

of history, just an immediate
need for materials.

Goethe sought more light and died.
Augustine needed more earth,
so overwrote Cicero, the Psalms
trumping but not undermining
De Republica, or so
the story went—

not unlike the Albert Speer bunker
in East Berlin, which the Russians
then next used to warehouse bananas from Cuba,
the redolence of which persisted in
the S&M techno club and now
the art gallery—four different stories
five stories deep

under *Reinhardtstrasse*—

unlike on the edge of our town,
where Digital Diversions Developers (3D)
does site preparation for DanteWorld,
the project beginning *in medias res*,
Purgatorio to open next fall.
The Inferno phase is fully financed,
but Paradiso is still dicey, if
not jagged,
and the architects struggle
to convert *terza rima* into glass,
steel, and rollercoasters.
La Vita Nuova Hotel and Spa
will open on schedule.

[Reload current page]

13

[The Speaker of Facts again:
"According to Wikipedia,
in the seventh century
the Dalai Lama dispatched
his scholars to Tibet's neighboring lands
and charged them to return
with a workable written language."]

(That 'pedia entry is subject, of course,
to revision, endless tweaking,

or deletion.
Check back
before speaking author-
itatively on this or any
other subject.)

At the Hot Links Café the wireless
is free. Every sausage tells a story,
and each like a story passes
through one grinder into another
in reaching the Reader's Digestion.

14

Meanwhile, in the Museum of Poetic Devices,
Ed Dorn's Literate Projector stands
on permanent display, running 24/7,
throwing transubstantiated movies
into stark text on a flat screen.
It purrs as the audience gasps
as "characters" become characters,
Brando's Terry Malloy's constellation
of movements and motives distilled
to combinations and recombinations
of 26 symbols and assorted punctuation,
diacritical marks and remarks

(My avatar's blog prevaricates:
Stephen wonders why the story
of Tibet's written language
has never been written
in Tibetan.)

contending for white space
and a reader's eye.
Crowds form to try to stump the Projector,
calling out *Andalusian Dog!* and *Three Stooges!*
and although it threw sparks
when distilling *Koyaanisqatsi,*
the text projected clear and linear
in the darkness of the filmic
transmutorium.

15

Stephen's avatar "writes": *Gravity*
obtains.

Bone House is no subterranean Berlin
banana bunker disco.
Bone House has but one story,
ground level, told over and over
and again,
but it has exactly as
many meanings
as the number of visitors
who pass through it.

On the walls of Bone House the Muralist
painted the story of human progress
under one old sun—

the hominid antecedents, agriculture,
the printed word, the modern flourish
of electromagnetic enterprise,
occupations, and pre-
occupations—

and the Muralist's descendants return
each generation to paint different faces,
pentimento, on Neanderthal,
homo habilis, statesman,
emperor, philosopher, and astronaut,
perfecting the belief in, while confirming,
the fallacy of perfectability.

"Stephen" blogs, *I'm not*
averse to avatars but I think
they should be seen, not
heard—no avatars
aloud—

16

I lie here writing in Bone House,
barely remembering First Life, when
the Word became flesh and the world
rippled out from my hand and eye
to horizons more easily imagined now
than understood then—

or when I sank into Second Life
and learned to look out
these windows, walk
these hallways, pace these empty rooms,
forget names and faces, and tear
the pages from the book of hours.

Words failing, flesh failing,
the world without
falling in while
the exhaust of the backhoe
mixes with the memory
of mortuary gardenias.

The nouns break down into
phonemes, then consonants, vowels,
then curved and straight lines, serifs,
dots, before dissolving
into the silent earth.
The verbs evaporate
in their own heated intensity.

I lie here writing in Bone House.
I lie and I wait.

17

At which "my" "avatar" "deletes"
"his" "story" and blinks at history,
all of which words
in the preceding clause
constitute a narrative,
notwithstanding
what any "narrator" in
good standing may tell us,

not unlike the habitual clicking
of the reload button—

410 Error: Gone

[Reload current page]

Ἐν ἀρχῃ ἦν ὁ Λογος.
Caveat lector.

About the Author

Stephen Bunch lives and writes in Lawrence, Kansas. From 1978 to 1988, he edited and published the little magazine *Tellus*, which featured local, regional, and nationally known writers. After a 15-year hiatus, he resumed writing in 2005. In 2008, he received the Langston Hughes Creative Writing Award for Poetry from Raven Books and the Lawrence Arts Center. His chapbook, *Preparing to Leave*, was published in 2011 by The Lives You Touch Publications.

www.ingramcontent.com/pod-product-compliance
Lightning Source LLC
Chambersburg PA
CBHW030156070426
42447CB00031B/682